Preach Cherisse

Inspirational Messages To Feed The Soul

BY CHERISSE STEPHENS

Preach Cherisse

Inspirational Messages To Feed The Soul

Published by Praisem Worldwide Publishing Company
© 2024 Cherisse Stephens
International Standard Book Number
979-8-218-48370-8

Scripture quotations are from
The Holy Bible, King James Version (KJV)
The Holy Bible, New International Version (NIV)
© 1973

Introduction

What's In Your GARDEN?

When I think of "Soul Food", I think of all the natural ingredients we can enjoy from a garden to include: Collard & Turnip Greens, Corn, Okra, Potatoes, Tomatoes, herbs, fruits and so much more. All of these ingredients will be enjoyed in a good ol fashioned meal. Many of us have recipes from our family members, like our Grandparents, Parents, Siblings and even good friends. If you're like me, you have recipes that have been passed down to you from generation to generation.

All the ingredients we plant, and grow in our gardens, will eventually be beneficial to us as we consume them in our daily intake of nutrients.

Well, just like we are intentional about eating foods naturally to help us grow strong and healthy, we should also consider what we're planting and consuming in our spiritual temple as well. The Bible gives us some good information about what to eat while we're on our spiritual walk. For example, the Fruit of the Spirit includes love, joy, peace, patience, kindness, generosity, faithfulness, gentleness and self control.

(Galatians 5:22-23).

These attributes can be the right ingredients to be used daily as we continue to develop into the character that will not only bless us, but those around us as well.

I pray that the words in this book of inspiration will help to nourish and FEED THE SOUL. While you will find passages of scripture to instruct and guide us, you'll also find some instructions and guidance from what I call my "Preach Cherisse Moments". It's just my take on life and how I've gotten through life with God and the Bible as my tour guide.

Thank God for the road map to victory given to us through the Word Of God!

Make sure you share something from this book entitled "Preach Cherisse", Inspirational Messages to Feed The Soul", with someone to help change their life for the better.

The messages I share in this book will be short, but powerful and life changing! "I Think I Will" get started!

Let's Go...

#PreachCherisse

I'll Have The Daily Special Please!

Favor, Blessings and Increase on the Side!

Daily He Loads Me With His Blessings.

#SoulFood

Food For Thought:

Your Seeds Are Growing.

Your Harvest Is Coming.

Your Faith Is Blooming.

#LiveWell

What Are You Hungry For:

He that Hungers and Thirsts After Righteousness…

Shall Be Filled.

#IAmFull

There Is A Bread That's Healthy and Good For YOU!

It's Called The Bread Of Life

I am the bread of life; whoever comes to me shall not hunger and whoever believes in me shall never thirst.
John 6:35

What Can I Eat?

"Therefore I tell you, do not worry about your life, what you will eat or drink; or about your body, what you will wear. Is not life more than food, and the body more than clothes?

Don't Worry, God's Got You Covered.

You're Not In Egypt But You're Not In Promise Either.

Don't Get Stuck In the Desert!

Keep It Moving!

All the bases are Loaded in Your Favor!

You're Back In The Game!

Time to Score & Win!

#IWin

STOP TALKING!

Work In Silence
Grow In Silence
Pray In Silence

Watch God Promote You In Public!

Anointed Privately
Blessed Publicly

I Will NOT Change My Posture to Make Others Comfortable!

Remain Steadfast, Unmovable, Always Abounding In the Work Of The Lord.

Stand Firm

Just Do IT!

Being Confident of this very thing, that HE who has begun a good work in you, will perfect it until the day of Christ Jesus.

Philippians 1:6

#IBelieve

Process

Your Process will Produce the Promise!

God is Developing you NOW to Expose You Later!

My Latter Will Be Greater than the Former

This is For Somebody:

KEEP GOING!

#PreachCherisse

#IThinkIWill

Keep Praying!

Your Intercession has Intercepted the Plan of The Enemy!

The Ball Is In Your Court!

If You Haven't Started: Start

Started: Keep Going

If You Quit - Start Again!

#PreachCherisse

Your Great Just Got Greater!

Your BIG Just Got Bigger!

Your Life Just Got Better!

Now Shout On That!

I'm Responding Differently This Season.

Don't Take It Personally.

It's NOT Personal, It's Purpose!

#PreachCherisse

This Is For YOU!

Go Where You're Celebrated And NOT Tolerated.

#PreachCherisse

#IThinkIWill

Somebody Catch This:

You Need God, Not Them!

#PreachCherisse

It's Still Going To Happen!

Don't Give Up and Don't Give In!

Wait On The Lord!

Once We Do What's Required, We Get Positive Results!

No Negativity Allowed!

#PreachCherisse

What God Is Doing In You and With You, has Nothing to DO with How People Feel About You, Or How They Support You.

So Be FREE!

If The Son Therefore Shall Make You Free, Ye Shall Be Free Indeed. John 8:36

If It Takes Up Space, But Has No Place, Then It Or They Have To Go!

No Extra Luggage Allowed.

#NoRoomOverHead

If You Can't Check It And You Can't Take It,

Then You MUST Get RID Of IT!

Take Only What's Necessary In This Season.

#LeaveIt

THEM: You've Changed

YOU: Yes
I Grew Up
I Leveled Up

&

GOD Showed UP!

#PreachCherisse

It's Not Over!

God Has Another MOVE.

But as it is written, Eye hath not seen, nor ear heard, neither have entered into the heart of man, the things which God has prepared for them that love him.

1 Corinthians 2:9

What Shall We Say To These things?

If GOD Is For Us, Who Can Be Against Us?

Romans 8:31

That's It. That's All.

Hey God's Cover-Girl

God Wants To Use You, No Matter What They Said Or Feel About YOU!

You've Got The Goods! Proverbs 31

#Valuable

The Same People Who Looked Over You Will Have To Look At You…When God Elevates You.

#PreachCherisse

Press & Pray In Order To Stay In The Race!

I press on to reach the end of the race and receive the heavenly prize for which God, through Christ Jesus, is calling us.

Philippians 3:14

Have You Been Enjoying Your Soul Food?

Why Not Feed Someone Else! Share A
"Preach Cherisse Moment"
On Social Media

#FeedTheSoul

Pray While You Wait

Learn While You Wait

Praise While You Wait

"I Think I Will"

You Only Need One!

One Divine Connection

One Open Door

One YES From God

Lord, Give Me That One!

Feast - No Famine

We Feast on the Abundant Food You Provide; You let us Drink from the River of Your Goodness.

Psalm 36:8

God Is Taking The No Names and Putting HIS Name On Them!

You Are Anointed Appointed Approved.

#PreachCherisse

And Let Us Not Be Weary In Well Doing. For In DUE SEASON, We Shall Reap, If We Faint Not.
Galatians 6:9

What Is Due You Is Coming To YOU!

#PreachCherisse

GOD Will Put YOUR Name In Rooms Where Your FEET Have NOT Yet Entered.

Somebody is Looking for YOU! Get Ready.

#PreachCherisse

Remember - Nobody Can Take Your Place.

Your Place Is Permanent!

#PreachGirl

Get In The Room And Take Your SEAT At The TABLE!

God Has Already Prepared A Place For YOU!

#PreachCherisse

Congratulations!

God Is Teaching You How To Handle People Who Can't Handle You!

Get A GRIP!

Welcome to the Winner's Circle.

Get Ready To Hear This Over & Over Again;

CONGRATULATIONS

#PreachCherisse

#IThinkIWill

Caution:

Make Sure Your Seatbelts Are Securely Fastened.

It's Time To Take OFF!

Let's Go!

FAST FORWARD

Get READY TO GO FURTHER - FASTER!

ARE YOU READY?

LET'S GO

Whether You Came Up

Going Up
Or
On The Come Up

It's Only Up From Here.

#PreachCherisse
#IThinkIWill

TRAVEL Rules:

Travel Light So You Don't Miss Your Flight.

Don't Try To Carry What Should Be Checked!

#CarryON

You Were In A Holding Pattern, But You Forgot That GOD Was Taking You Higher While Holding!

#PreachCherisse

Be Careful & Prayerful About People Who Have An Attitude About Your Altitude!

If They Are Afraid To FLY - Say Goodbye!

Higher Lord!

You're About To Birth What You've Been Carrying.

Get Ready for Multiples!

Double For Your Trouble.

#SayThat

Recompense Is Coming.

God Is Going To:
Compensate
Indemnify
Repay
And
Reimburse You

Receive IT!

Payday Is On The Way!

Zelle
CashApp
Checking Account
Savings Account
Direct Deposits
Wire Transfers

It's Called
OVERFLOW!

Company's Coming:

Weeping May Endure For A Night, But JOY Is Coming In the Morning!

Good Morning!

#PreachCherisse

Access Granted

Behold, I set before you an OPEN DOOR That No Man Can Shut!

Revelation 3:8

#PreachCherisse

Obscurity Is A Prerequisite for Destiny.

God Knows My Name.

#PreachCherisse

The Gift Of A Person Will Open Doors For Him, And Before The Great, It Gives Him Access.

Proverbs 18:16

In This Season Of Your Life:

Follow Directions And NOT Distractions.

#PreachCherisse #IThinkIWill

Remember This:

You Don't Need Proof, When You've Got the Promise!

God Said It And That Settles It.

#Period

This Will Be Your Declaration:

God Has Done It AGAIN!

Blessings
Healing
Salvation
Opportunities
Favor

Walk It Out!

When The Blessing Comes, You Won't Have Time To Explain What It's About.

Just Walk It Out!

#IThinkIWill

Somebody Shout

Paid In FULL!

God Has Already Done It.

Glory To God.

#AllExpensesPaid

Check Your Temperature Before You Try To Set Someone Else's Thermostat.

Read Matthew 7:5

#Ouch

God Will Use The One They Least Expected!

You Were Least Likely To Succeed, But God Has Blessed You Indeed!

Shout I'm Blessed!

#PreachCherisse

Declare This Blessing:

Yes Indeed, It Won't Be Long Now, God's Decree. Things Are Going To Happen so fast your head will swim, one thing fast on the heels of the other. You won't be able to keep up. Everything will be happening at once-and everywhere you look, blessings! Blessings like wine pouring off the mountains and hills. I'll make everything right again for my people Israel:

They'll rebuild their ruined cities. They'll plant vineyards and drink good wine. They'll work their gardens and eat fresh vegetables. And I'll plant them, plant them on their own land. They'll never again be uprooted from the land I've given them. God, your God, says so.

Amos 9:13-15

67

Don't Try To Fit In With The Crowd.

There Will Be Separation Before Elevation.

#PreachCherisse

Just Because You're Alone, Doesn't Mean You're Lonely.

God Is Always With You.

#PreachCherisse

Your Inner Circle Should Love You and Like You.

Some People Love What You Do, But Hate That It's You.

#PreachCherisse #IDid

GOD is Providing You With Vision Pushers, Not Vision Snatchers.

They See You, Acknowledge You and Celebrate You.

Push & Celebrate!

Remember –

The Blessings Of The Lord Are Yes and Amen.

Encourage Someone Today.

It Sounds Crazy Until It Happens!

Shout - I've Got CRAZY FAITH

Speak It Until You SEE It.

#IThinkIWill

Aren't You Glad That You're Covered By The Blood of Jesus?

No Weapon Formed Against You Shall Prosper.

Isaiah 54:17

Dress For Success

"Put on the whole armour of God, that ye may be able to stand against the wiles of the devil. For we wrestle not against flesh and blood, but against principalities, against powers, against the rulers of the darkness of this world, against spiritual wickedness in high places."
Ephesians 6: 11-12

The Faithful Are About to Become Fruitful.

Go Get Your Blessings!

#TimeToEat

Did You Know That You Are The Apple Of God's Eye?

He Loves You So Much.

Oh How He Loves Us!

Don't Retaliate

GOD Is Fighting For You.

Be Still And See The Salvation Of The Lord!

It's A Fixed Fight.

Don't Get Stuck In The Valley Of The Shadow Of Death.

Get To "I Will Fear No Evil, for Thou Art With Me".

#ThankGod

Your Last Season Qualified You For This NEW SEASON.

No Apologies Or Explanations Needed.

#Qualified
&
#Satisfied

THEM:
They Counted You Out.

YOU:
They Can't Count

12345678
2345678
345678
45678
5678
678
78
8

#CountYourBlessings

Life Insurance:

"For God So Loved The World, That He Gave His One And Only Son, That Whoever Believes In Him, Shall Not Perish, But Have Eternal Life".

John 3:16 (NIV)

Make Sure You're Covered.

The Rest Of Your Days Will Be The BEST Of Your Days!

Thank You God!

#Rest

God's Got Time Up Until It's Time.

Because He Created Time.

He's Not Moved By Our Timeline!

#WatchGod

What The Enemy Meant For Your BAD, God Has Already Turned It For Your GOOD!

Now Go Have A GOOD DAY!

#GoodDay

#PreachCherisse

God Is Taking RUSH ORDERS!

You've Waited Patiently, Now Get Ready To Receive Immediately.

#PlaceYourOrder

#SuperSizeIt

You're Going From The BACK to the Front.

From The Bottom To The Top.

God Has Flipped It!

#PreachCherisse

When God Elevates You, Nobody Can Separate You From The Promotion That's Coming Your Way!

I'm All The Way UP!

God is giving you 20/20 Vision
And
100 % Provision
For Your VISION

However, as it is written: "What no eye has seen, what no ear has heard, and what no human mind has conceived" – the things God has prepared for those who love him.

1 Corinthians 2:9

God Is Preserving You To Protect You!

But When He Releases You, You'll Be Better Than Before!

#PreserveMeGod

#PreachCherisse

Some Of My Favorite Songs:

Lord - While On Others Thou Art Calling - Do Not Pass Me By!

I Need Thee Oh I Need Thee, Every Hour, I need Thee. Oh Bless Me Now, My Savior... I Come To Thee.

Sing Your Favorite Songs Today!

Your Results Are In…

You Passed The Test!

Congratulations Again.

#NoRetakesNecessary

Remember - God Can Only Bless The Real You.

He Will NOT Bless Who You Pretend To BE.

Be True To YOU!

Did I Preach?

Your Nutrition Facts

Love	100%
Joy	100%
Peace	100%
Patience	100%
Kindness	100%
Goodness	100%
Faithful	100%
Gentle	100%
Mercy	100%
Grace	100%
Hope	100%
Self Control	100%
Restoration	100%
Forgiveness	100%

Bon Appetit

You've Been Eating Well And It Shows!

Your Countenance Is Bright And Your Shine Is Real.

Keep Digesting The Word Of God.

You Are Stronger Now! You Have The Strength To Climb Mountains.

#MountainClimber

Alright Now! It's Time To Go Higher!

See You At The TOP Cause The BOTTOM Is Too Crowded.

I'm Ready For the Climb!

We All The Way UP!

You Should Be So Very Proud Of Yourself.

You've Planted Beautiful Things In Your Garden That Feed Your Soul.

Keep Sowing & Growing.

#YouReapWhatYouSow

Now that you're spiritually full from all the "Soul Food", make sure you share the recipes in this book! You can do so, by purchasing books for those you know and love.

Pass the Plate and Feed Someone Else, Some Good Ol "Soul Food".

#PreachCherisse
**Order Books From Cherisse Stephens,
Online And Wherever Books Are Sold.**

For Booking:
CherisseStephensFoundation.Com
CherisseStephensMinistries@Gmail.Com

Facebook
PreachCherisse
Cherisse Stephens
GodsCoverGirls

Instagram
Cherisse Stephens
GodsCoverGirls
Cherisse Is On

YouTube
Cherisse Is On